by Shirley Frederick

 Harcourt

Orlando   Austin   Chicago   New York   Toronto   London   San Diego

Visit *The Learning Site!*
www.harcourtschool.com

Turtles are reptiles

Like snakes and lizards, turtles are reptiles. They are ectothermic, which means their body temperature is about the same as the air or water around them. Sea turtles live in the ocean. Their legs are like paddles, and they are good swimmers. Unlike land turtles, sea turtles cannot pull their legs and head into their shell. However, they do carry their house on their back, and it's a big house. An adult green sea turtle can weigh as much as 330 lbs. (150 kg) and its top shell can be over 3 feet (91 cm) long.

Green sea turtles are reptiles that have been around since before dinosaurs walked the earth.

Turtles are fascinating creatures. Slow on land and graceful in the sea, they carry their boxy homes with them wherever they go. Turtles are gentle creatures. At one time, there were millions of sea turtles living in the Gulf of Mexico. Over the years, though, the number has been going down. All sea turtles in the Gulf of Mexico are now endangered, or threatened with extinction. Scientists are trying to change this by protecting and studying sea turtles.

Calling All Turtles!

What happened to all those turtles? That's what scientists are trying to find out. They know that for hundreds of years people hunted turtles. Some people used turtles as a source of food. The beautiful shells of hawksbill turtles were used for eyeglass frames, combs, and jewelry. Turtles were caught and sold as pets. Today it is against the law in the United States to capture sea turtles or sea turtle eggs.

Sea turtles live in water, but they lay their eggs on land. In the spring or summer a female sea turtle will crawl up on a beach to lay her eggs. With her flippers she digs a hole in the sand. Then she lays her eggs in the hole. A set of sea turtle eggs is called a clutch. A female sea turtle can lay several clutches of eggs during a season. After laying the eggs, the turtle covers them up. In this time, she may lay up to 1,000 eggs. Tiny turtles develop inside the eggs while they are in the sand.

The turtles that come out of the eggs are called hatchlings. After the hatchlings are born they head straight for the water. How do they know which way to go? Scientists think that they look for light. If they are born at night, the turtles look for the moon and moonlight on the water. If they hatch during the day, they look for sunlight over the water. Even scientists are surprised by how the hatchlings find their way. "It's amazing to see these tiny animals scurry to the water," says Dr. Donna Shaver-Miller, an expert on sea turtles. "They have no help from their mothers. Yet they know where to go."

Sea turtles travel long distances from their feeding grounds back to their nesting beach. It will be another three years before the same female nests again.

No Place Like Home

Most sea turtles lay their eggs on the same beach where they were born. To get there, they may have to travel long distances. Why do they do this? How do they find the beach? No one knows for sure, not even scientists.

From the very start, a sea turtle's life is difficult. Even when a clutch has hundreds of eggs, only a few hatchlings survive. Predators, or animals that eat the turtles, are waiting. While the eggs are still in the sand, hungry skunks, raccoons, or sea crabs may dig them up.

It takes a female sea turtle about 25 years before she is mature enough to lay eggs.

Hatchlings struggle with their flippers and wriggle their bodies to get out of their shells.

People watch as a mother turtle makes her way back into the ocean.

If the turtles hatch during the day, seagulls may dive down and grab them. In the ocean, fish can snap them up.

A group of female turtles nesting at the same time is called an *arribada,* which means "arrival" in Spanish. Scientists think there's a good reason why turtles nest at the same time. If a large number of hatchlings are born at the same time, more will survive. A predator can eat only so many in one day.

Even adult sea turtles face many dangers. Some turtles get tangled in fishing nets. The leatherback sea turtle is sometimes hurt by eating trash. Some turtles eat jellyfish, but a turtle can mistake a plastic bag for a jellyfish. Trash in a turtle's stomach can be deadly. By learning more about the kinds of things that can hurt turtles, scientists hope they can better protect them in the future.

Many people work hard to protect sea turtles. Padre Island National Seashore on the southern coast of Texas is one place where turtles are protected. There, scientists and other people work together to help sea turtles.

Of all the sea turtles at Padre Island, the Kemp's ridley sea turtle is the smallest. It is named after Richard Kemp, a fisher who first spotted the turtle in 1880. Kemp's ridley sea turtles are about 25 inches (64 cm) long and weigh about 100 pounds (45 kg). They are also the most endangered of all sea turtles.

At one time, people who fished thought that Kemp's ridley sea turtles didn't lay eggs. That's because the fishers didn't know where to look. In 1947 a film was made of nesting Kemp's ridleys. The film showed about 40,000 turtles nesting on the same day.

Concerned people began an effort to help the turtles. They decided to start a protected nesting place for the Kemp's ridley. Padre Island National Seashore was chosen because it is in a national park, and it is a safe place for turtles.

This hatchling is now big enough to be released in the ocean.

From 1978 to 1988 Kemp's ridley eggs were brought from Mexico to Padre Island National Seashore. The hatchlings were released on the beach. Scientists knew the hatchlings would remember the site. As adults, some females might come back and lay eggs there.

The hatchlings made it to the water, but they were not yet free. To study and help them, scientists collected the turtles and took them to a building in Galveston, Texas. The turtles were placed in buckets and fed trout chow—a kind of turtle food. Schoolchildren had donated money to buy the chow. The turtles were fed until they were a year old. By then, they were large enough to live in the ocean.

There is safety in numbers on Padre Island National Seashore. Here a large batch of sea turtles is released on the protected beach in the hopes that, as adults, the females will return to lay eggs.

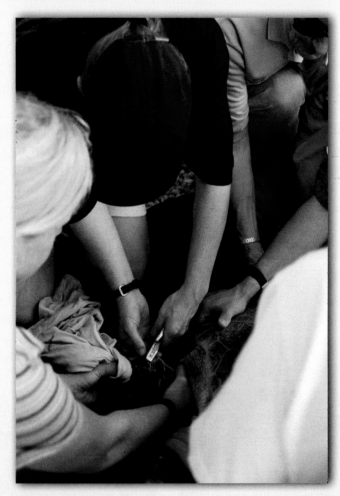

Scientists tag a turtle on Padre Island for tracking purposes.

Tag, You're It!

Scientists and their helpers attached a metal tag to a front flipper of each of the year-old turtles. Some of the little turtles were also marked with living tags. A tiny piece of light-colored shell was removed from each animal's bottom shell. The piece was placed in a small hole drilled in the darker top shell and held there with a special kind of glue. This tag was easy to see and would last the life of the turtle.

When all the turtles had been tagged, they were set free into the Gulf of Mexico. Then they were on their own. Their chances for survival had improved, which is why this program was called head-start.

Did the head-start program work? Scientists were eager to find out, but they had to be patient. It takes 10 to 15 years for a Kemp's ridley turtle to grow up. The good news came in 1996. Two turtles with living tags nested at the national seashore. Since then, 10 head-start turtles have nested on or near Padre Island.

Turtles at the national seashore don't have much of a private life, which is a very good thing. During turtle nesting time, people are watching. Volunteers and park workers patrol the beach, looking for nesting turtles. Beach visitors also find them and report their locations. When a nest is found, the eggs are placed in boxes. The eggs are taken to an incubation room, where they are safe.

Scientist Donna Shaver-Miller digs up turtle eggs from a nest to help hatchlings have a better chance at survival.

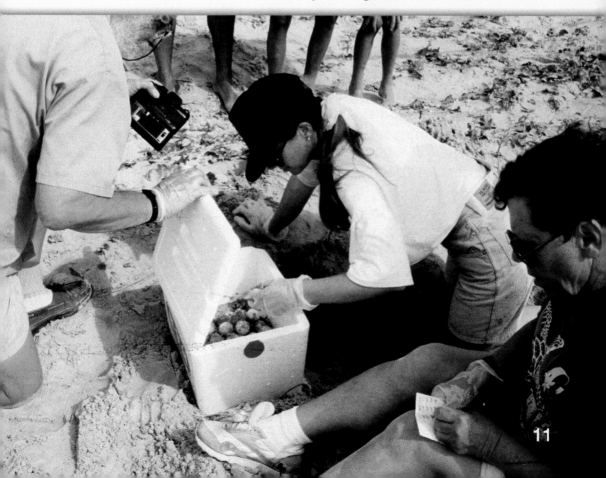

Once the turtles have hatched, they are released on the beach. Children and other visitors come to watch. A turtle release is a special event. "Few people ever get to see this. Seeing it is a chance of a lifetime," says Donna Shaver-Miller. "It's important that kids learn about sea turtles. They learn best when they actually get a chance to see the turtles. These children are the ones who will be saving sea turtles in the future."

Volunteers make sure that seagulls and crabs do not eat the turtles. "Finding and raising baby turtles is a lot of work," says Shaver-Miller, who has done it for several years. "We do not have enough money to pay all the people needed. The success of our program depends on our volunteers."

Many of those volunteers are busy teaching others about sea turtles. They put information on the Internet and visit schools. Scientists are busy, too. They want to learn more about sea turtles. How far do they travel? Where do they feed? How do they find their way in the ocean? To learn these things, scientists collect information about where the turtles are and what they are doing. But how do you watch a turtle that is somewhere in a very big ocean?

This hatchling has a long, dangerous road ahead as it starts its life as a sea turtle.

Ways to help turtles

1. Cut back on the amount of plastic you use.
2. Tell people how harmful helium balloons can be. They may end up in the ocean, where sea turtles might mistake them for food.
3. Write a letter to the editor of your local newspaper telling about these dangers.
4. If you live near the coast, encourage your family to turn off beachfront lights during turtle nesting season. The lights confuse the turtles.
5. Read more about programs you can join to help sea turtles. Many projects have Web sites.

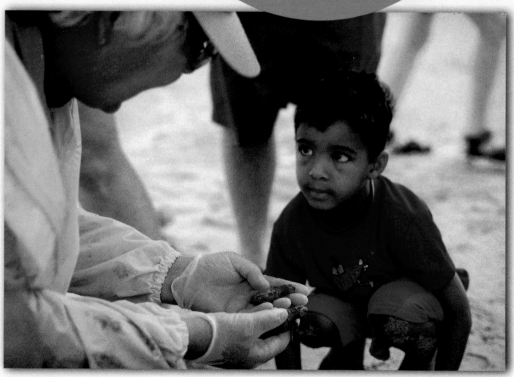

A volunteer teaches a child how to keep baby sea turtles safe.

Help from Up Above

Satellites help in tracking turtles. Scientists have attached satellite transmitters to the shells of some sea turtles. A turtle has to come up to the surface to breathe. Then its transmitter is out of the water and can send out signals. Satellites high above Earth receive signals from the transmitters. Scientists use computers to help them figure out the information they are receiving from the satellites. This helps them know where the turtles are. If the scientists are lucky, they get information from the same turtle two days in a row. Then they can tell how far and how fast the turtle has traveled. Sometimes sea turtles stay in the same area for many days. This could mean they are feeding or getting ready for nesting.

A park ranger makes sure this turtle's tracking device is correctly attached.

The satellites and transmitters don't work perfectly. Sometimes a transmitter falls off the turtle. Sometimes it stops working. Sometimes a turtle comes up for air when no satellite is overhead. Even so, scientists are learning a lot about sea turtles.

A satellite tracks turtles that have transmitters attached to their shells.

Why is it important to save the sea turtles? Plants and animals depend on one another. If one kind of plant or animal becomes extinct, or dies out, others will be affected. Each plant and animal has an important place in the web of life. Those who work to protect sea turtles want to make sure these gentle creatures never lose their place.